NOTE FROM T

Welcome to the new issue of Ibbetson Street. In this issue we have the work of Ted Kooser, Marge Piercy, X. J.Kennedy, Kathleen Spivack, Mary Buchinger Bodwell, and many others. You will notice Dianne Robitaille's accomplished photography adorning our front cover and the artwork of longtime contributor Bridget Galway on the back cover.

We are also glad to include an interview with Pulitzer-Prize-winning novelist Paul Harding conducted by Endicott College undergraduate Nicole Cadro.

Ibbetson Street remains visible and active. Recently we have released new chapbooks by talented Endicott College undergraduates Daniel Goodwin and Alex Munteanu under the Ibbetson Street Press/Endicott College Young Poet Series and we plan to release a full-length collection by poet Keith Tornheim this summer. Emily Pineau, our director, is doing a fine job working with our emerging poets.

The Ibbetson Street Press/Endicott College Visting Author Series continues to thrive. This spring we had master storyteller Sebastian Lockwood, and the acclaimed novelist Paul Harding as guests.

We want to thank our Poetry Editor Harris Gardner, our Co-Managing Editor, Lawrence Kessenich, and Designer Steve Glines for putting together this issue. And, as always, we thank Endicott College for their continued support.

—Doug Holder, 2016

Ibbetson Street Press
25 School St.
Somerville, MA 02143

Publisher: Doug Holder
Managing Editors: Lawrence Kessenich, Rene Schwiesow
Poetry Editor: Harris Gardner
Consulting Editors: Robert K. Johnson, Dianne Robitaille, Emily Pineau
Art Consultant: Richard Wilhelm
Design: Steve Glines
Website Manager: Steve Glines
Front cover photograph by Dianne Robitaille and back cover art by Bridget Galway

Boston Area Small Press and Poetry Scene http://dougholder.blogspot.com
Doug Holder's CV: http://dougholderresume.blogspot.com
Ibbetson Street Press http://ibbetsonpress.com
ISCS PRESS http://www.iscspress.com
Ibbetson Street Press Online Bookstore http://www.tinyurl.com/3x6rgv3

The Ibbetson Street Press is supported by and formally affiliated with Endicott College, Beverly,
Massachusetts. http://www.endicott.edu

No simultaneous submissions; no poems previously published in print or online. All submissions
must be sent by email only to tapestryofvoices@yahoo.com—as an attachment or pasted into the
body of the email.

CONTENTS

THE CAFE

No one but old people here,
each at a separate table.
Rain streams down outside
among the sycamores: the
little dim cafe steams over.

Time has clouded this
fought-over village,
its public square and
streets and bicycles.
Each war has stripped France
of its sperm pool: women
sit alone and testify;

clutching small glasses of absinthe,
reproaches, and the waste of
possibility. A heater sizzles,
puddles of rain form on the floor,
and what was beautiful
is glazed by rain and dreary.
Leaves flatten themselves
on the cobbled streets.

Useless leaves, leftover
five fingered leaves;
"...*comme Il pleut dans mon coeur.....*"
a subdominant theme, the
true National Anthem.
"Military" and "Losses,"
these twinned words,
have married in the cemetery grove
beyond wrought iron gates

flanked by a huge naked
statue of "La Victoire:" France as
a blossoming full-bosomed virgin.
And in the town, small
hunched ladies wait, staring
unblinking into solitude,
their papery hands, fine veined,
fallen forever upon half empty glasses.

—*Kathleen Spivack*

VISITING JERUSALEM

I trip and scrape my knee
on a cobblestone,
leaving a little blood on the curb.

*

In a packed café,
I'm mumbling
a warning to myself about cafés.

*

The stabbings are elsewhere.
The stabbings are in another
part of the city, where I'm not.

*

Come into my shop, he says,
come look at the necklaces,
the rings.

*

How long
have I been the enemy?
What god am I counting on?

*

A hundred times a day I touch
my passport in my pocketbook
just to make sure my hand's still there.

—*Jennifer Barber*

THE PURPOSE OF THE WORLD

Evan sat by a window in California
Through it he watched a cat in the grass.
It was stalking something invisible to him.

In Kentucky Belle stood on the bank of a river.
A warm breeze patterned the surface.
A dragonfly coursed above the brown water.

At Santa Maria's entrance the day dragged.
Esma sat inches from the feet of strangers.
She hunched head down, feet bare, hand out.

The American President spoke to the press.
Cameras flashed ceaselessly.
He announced a new weapon system.

Belle saw the dragonfly describe the same circle.
No, not quite the same.
It ballooned, it shrank, it shifted.

The man from Uganda sweated in his cab.
The line of taxis edged slowly forward.
New York: better money, worse air.

The cat was watching a spot in the tall grass.
Finally there was movement and she pounced.
Evan thought about writing a letter.

The President said the nation needed protection.
He used his most serious voice.
"It's a perilous world; we need to meet the challenge."

It was the third day of the earthquake rescue.
Hope had grown thin.
Kai Xi was almost faint from hunger.

Esma had been begging for ten years now.
Almost always lately in this spot.
Some days she managed to hold up her head.

Xi had not slept except for two hours.
He'd slept then like someone dead.
He'd eaten only two small meals.

The President also addressed the economy.
He was glad to report good news for the middle class.
He wanted to mention the poor, but felt he couldn't.

2

Solomon wasn't sure he should have left Uganda.
Yet there had seemed nothing for which to stay.
Perhaps he would meet a woman here, and marry.

The dragonfly curved and swerved above the water,
catching tiny insects, almost never missing.
Belle loved how its wings shone in the sun.

Xi had begun to think of taking a break
but he heard a faint voice, the voice of a child.
His weariness gone, he called out and began to dig.

Esma knew today she'd bring nothing home.
The pain and cramps were all she could think of.
The heat, the tourists' voices were too much.

Evan would start the letter with the cat but
more importantly it would express his regret—
he would ask his old friend to forgive him.

—*Kathleen Lentz*

AS WITH POEM

as with trembling, a cloud that veils
a hand, as with shaking, a mist in
the grass

as with murmuring, a voice
calls the name of a friend

listening, the stone rises like
a star

caressing, the lips
tremble

crying, the veiled
message delivers

here we stand, waiting for honey
and the dark stain of the wise

we gather like strangers who seem
to know one another

at daybreak,
what kind of blessing will come?

—*Judy Katz-Levine*

DREAM DANCERS

when my dreams become dancers
and my spirit sucks the nectar of
the melting of the sun and the sky

when the redness/orangey of that ball
makes me be grateful to be alive

when my body grates the peace
that my meditations embrace

when I awaken to the present moment
in the silence of the birds in the brushing of
the leaves of the trees by the wind

when I enter that white space where
I forge my physical pains
and my soul's old wounds

when I glow shaking my preconceived ideas
about being the apparent me

when the mask I wear and the role I play
on this earth vanishes

     I   melt onto one
     I   melt onto all

          —Beatriz Alba del Rio

RED APPLES

It was September, me and the girls
had two budgies and hope.

We waited, ate the apples, lived.
We gathered stuff around us
that winter and were ready
in Spring for the baby.

Every Autumn I look out
at those apples and remember.

          —Triona McMorrow

BRIEF ENCOUNTER

Her eyes were bright as eyes might ever be,
Gray hair swept back and neatly knotted tight,
Her face lined with the soft geometry
Of age, the chances of our greeting slight.
Yet when I looked to her she looked at me,
We smiled as she walked down to keep her day
Where I had come to swim and now to leave.
Just for a moment neither turned away
As if we could, had circumstance allowed
Us both to speak, have gentle words to say
To one another, the smallest seeds sowed
In a willing field, willing in that way
Of nature's dark embrace to bring them to
A flowering. Yet both of us were old
Enough to understand demands to go
Our separate ways, perhaps to hold
This brief encounter, eye-to-eye, within
Knowing, unknown hearts, an intimacy,
Whose early morning's passing would begin
The day imagining what could not be.

          —Philip E. Burnham, Jr.

THE REAL THING

A glimpse in the shop as I buy porridge,
I jump with my heart, blindly count
out money, mouth dry, hands aflutter.
Did he see me? He is busy putting his stuff
 into an old peoples shopping bag.

But we are older , not like when we collided
and were intertwined for a winter in the nineties.
I want to walk to him, is he still married? I'll ask.
I don't. Instead, I buy a pair of suede boots
in Penneys for a fiver.I am over it now.

          —Triona McMorrow

I NEVER REALLY
TRUSTED YOU

There it is, ink to paper
crisp edges, no bleeding
into the white
space inside the program
where you planted nightmares

and I woke in fear.

I acknowledge
that the vivid 3 am terrors
may have come
from my own hands—
I admit to the dirt beneath my nails.

The bell chimes. There is no dinner.
There never has been.

You kept me in a glass jar,
my small fists silenced,
you tap, tap, tapping

success on a keyboard
where you wrote about the curve,
the rise and fall
of each measured move,

and I doubled over
from the sucker punch.

—*Rene Schwiesow*

IT'S NOT ONLY IN HER
DREAMS THE MAD GIRL IS
TURNING INTO CINDERELLA

the gray days have dogged
her for years, each day
scrubbing the cat box, the mounds
of polished silver. Her hair
hangs greasy and lank. She vacuums
loss by the hour. If there was some
one to talk to. If someone knew
her name but the others don't
see past their gold plated
Lamborghinis and diamonds. But
the mad girl knows before the
moon is eclipsed, turns blood red
and vermilion, she will step
from her tattered rags, rinse
sadness and shame from
her as she washes the dust and
grease from her curls that suddenly
are golden and pops two drugs
as she slithers into silk and lace and
rhinestone shoes and dashes
to the ball where for as
long as she's able, as long as
the pills and magic hold
she will fly thru arms that couldn't
imagine her not as a beauty
until the feels the magic
start to go, the wicked hour sliding
closer when all the beauty
goes away and even if
she hasn't lost a shoe or had some
prince of a man follow and
find her she feels the
high fade away and tears her
Dolce Gabanna she'll never wear
again shredded and stained
as she will feel
by dawn

—*Lyn Lifshin*

YOU RETURN TO ME

you return to me because I am the fish
whose face you remember because the sea
-weed is clearing past its slimy obfuscation
because as if in a dream of clouds and water
there is a clearing and the bell of a name
danielle you call because now I am the daughter
who sat on your lap and cracked a noisy joke
and made you laugh the one who turns the key
because you are someone to me who reaches
through the tunnel who turns the sound down
and tells the nurses you are not only this

when the window scratches the tree outside
next to it and the anchor of the television
is only behind the mesh of the screen you
are my star nonetheless even through
the white noise and the ring sewn
onto my hand and the heart
in my pocket

—Danielle Legros-George

COMMENTS FROM THE DISPLACED

Friends unheard from in thirty years
pop up on Facebook commenting on photos
of my cats or garden or just me.

We all trot through life dragging
skeins of relationships that have fallen
into disrepair, gotten snagged on

quarrels, just forgotten like a trowel
left in the garden to rust. Sometimes
I'm pleased to hear from one who made

a sojourn in a bleak place bearable.
Sometimes it's just a pen turning
up with the ink dried and useless.

Sometimes they bring back old pain--
something amputated that can hurt
as if it were still attached.

—Marge Piercy

WHERE YOUR PHONE RANG

1. I remember: Home
   was where your phone rang.
   Every time you moved
   a new number,
   another set of voices.

2. It's where you hid the shell
   of the horseshoe crab
   on the path behind the garage,
   among the blackberry bushes
   and their thorns.

3. Your children waited for you on a porch—
   first one, then another, then three.
   You pitched underhand in the front yard
   until the sky, horsehair gray,
   fell all around you.

4. Home was where the creaking of the trees outside
   played see-saw with your breath,
   where the book bounced
   off your chest and slipped to the floor,
   and the whiskey cabinet's door yawned wide.

5. Now whether there's wind on your face,
   or the wind's to your back,
   the sky's a color you always recognize,
   come morning, come night,
   even as it changes.

—Tim Kinsella

JUNE AFTERNOON

The sky is all covered with cobwebs,
wisps of them, drifting so high
that probably no one could reach them
with a rag on a broom, and not a soul
is trying. How did it come to this?
Hundreds of people with time on their hands
and not one broom in the air!

—Ted Kooser

POEM FOR FRED MARCHANT

The first purple,
honey mustard shock trooper
crocuses come up.
clear sidewalks,
and nothing but intimations—
then a quick snow,
and by late afternoon,
the group of Chinese kids
move the basketball
around on the court
in front of the big igloo
town skating rinks,
some sporty characters
who got the spirit
must have been driving by—
baseball caps
and dress shoes
and pants, the two guys
and the girl
in her furry boots,
but, ah, still graceful.
Inside the third graders
learn to glide
on one skate
while winter goes.
As Fred knows,
Heaney knew nobody
happy can remain
utterly sophisticated.
There must be a moment
to gaze into your cat's face
and see the small cat
boogers in the dark
runnels of wet nose,
after the feints
and evasions that allow
other things,
the purely organic
and manmade, to grow.

—David Blair

ON A POEM FROM DAVID BLAIR

A major accident, it says, down
on Pleasant Street, a bannered
e-mail alert that comes in on top
of many things I don't want to
know or picture. Then something
I do not expect arrives pinging,
a purple nub that pokes through
our winter mess like Williams'
wild-cabbage leaf, works its way
up through the debris of polls,
evasions, and arrogance, a poem
in which your child Astrid skates
on the edge of one blade, and boys
pile out of a car and begin a game
of horse on a winter-empty court.
A poem in which your cat purrs
through its soft, slightly crusted
nose, the air carrying to its mind
the sparrow it watches, assessing,
a set of cat-neurons on which nothing
is lost from all that is given, a mind
that moves with sleek, sure-footed
shivers of recognition. An image
of how the poem enters or passes
through us, sparking off a feeling
we don't have a name for yet, but
we know is pure gift, a total freebie.

—Fred Marchant

YESTERDAY AND TOMORROW

Overhead the whine of a plane; the day heats up—
picture book blue sky, puff of clouds.

Here is the deep magic, the daemon that transforms,
the muse, wood spirit-angel, the outlaw,
the out of bounds creature. No fence, or border wall
can keep them in or out; they hitch rides
on tumble weeds, stray sand or wood mice—wherever
the wind blows; dust-devils dance, whirl
in doorways on grates, under bridges.
Foxes have holes, but these sleep
the sleep of the wanderer under hedges.
They watch the stars, the turtles by the pond in the park;
they listen to frogs thrum far from
the subway rattle, and the ache for yesterday's dream—
that once, time was simple, possible to hold fast.
Each day the sun rose to coffee and toast; the pattern held.
Now in flux, up is down, across the town some-
where else; and no one knows who is
who as they slither and slide in a bright world of chance.
Perhaps today is a lucky day.

In sudden rain pigeons step dainty-footed through puddles;
the gutter rushes sticks and trash to the drain.

A small boy wonders.

—Molly Mattfield Bennett

REMEMBERED PLACES

My mother never drove past her grammar school in the next town without pointing it out to us.
My father liked to walk the holes of the old municipal course he'd played
As a boy, his seven iron doubling as walking stick and putter.
I drive down roads to the same beaches and woods I did as a teen,
But I don't get out to see what's changed.
We go back to places to be in them like favorite clothing
And feel again the confidence we had young. Here, we can't be lost;
We know the light, that line of trees, that small incline, the sounds.
We stay until others wonder where we are.

—William Harney

WHEN I THINK OF MY CHILDHOOD

I think of family, a picture
we hold together perhaps
a painting, the one of fruit

in a bowl. Sometimes when I stare,
I swear I see the soft parts turn
bad, the bruises. On the playground

every apparatus brought fearful results
The jungle gym, my throat choked at a bar
a see-saw comrades leapt off I sat at the top
of a slide, punched all the way to the bottom

At age sixteen, a hundred forty pounds
an empty pit, my ribs stuck out like a step ladder
my toothpick arms with bulbous hinges
I think it impossible to fill my stomach
not that we were wanting, just a never ending

well… To think—was I saved by my
great escapes? I had to come back from
those years later when the Merry-go-round spun
me dry, I woke up late that morning,
still no longer a boy subsisting

living in my head was easy to do, with nothing
to do—the smoke you see raging from my ears
is just my image in the mirror, made quite a sight
of myself. I hoped to be different

—*Timothy Gager*

GREENWICH VILLAGE 1959

Hudson and Jane
Our five big rooms
brick walled kitchen
the window over
a double porcelain sink.
I was small for bathing in,
then climb through
to our tar beach roof.

Hot and sticky breezeless summer-
Coke bottle collecting for penny candy.
Running towards the King Kong Ride,
and ice cream truck.

Hanging with the Fernandez family,
ten brothers and sisters
Strong in number.
Open came the hydrant,
 in that city waterfall we played.

Sheridan Square,
Charlie bum Jimmy bum,
all harmless and sweet.
Watched us with droopy eyes and crooked
smiles,
 play hopscotch and bottle caps.

 Washington Square
 playground and tall slide.

 Old men gathered
 playing chess
 in custom hats,
 orthodox, or tweed caps.

Beatniks on benches
smoking, talking jive.

Children splashed in the fountain pool.
Music with chorus of pigeon's coo
All this jumbled in a tumbler of sound.

I would lie under an elder tree
look up through the patchwork of sky and
leaves.
It was then and there I felt everything,
And everything was old and new
When the breeze came.

—Bridget Seley-Galway

CLIMB

As a child I sat in the backyard
hours: here a black ant lugged
a crumb a robin dropped from bread
my mother scattered from the door;

there a bee walked on and under
a clover blossom like my mother
picking over peaches at the market,
or looking through her junk drawer,

searching first here then there for
something precious she misplaced.
But how do I find what was lost
when I abandoned my mother

and took my father's hard hand
to switchback up history's crag,
his understanding already bloodied
by desperately certain stakes

and mine by my fear of weakness?
We clattered up the treacherous path,
our distance from home precisely
the sum of what escaped our notice.

—Richard Hoffman

NICHOLAS

Just born, still swaddled in umbilical cord,
Nicholas leaped to his feet, cried "Praise the Lord!"—
A fast start. Once when a hard-up neighbor
Couldn't raise dowries, only sinful labor
Loomed for his daughters till the good saint tossed
Into their bed a ball of purest gold,
Rescuing them from being bought and sold;
And when a vile inn-keeper, soused on wine,
Figuring human victims to be cheaper
Than beef to feed his guests, butchered three boys
And soaked their bodies in a vat of brine,
It took the godly Nicholas to revive
Them with a blessing, bring 'em back alive
With salt tastes in their mouths, but no regrets—
A miracle to be remembered. Let's
Seek refuge in the bosom of Saint Nicholas
Should anybody ever try to pickle us.

—*X. J. Kennedy*

FROM A LOST POEM

Haircutless, shaveless, wineless lifter of weights,
Samson, even before his birth, was allotted his life by a nameless angel.
Heroes do have a way of being marked from the cradle or earlier,
like Jacob and Moses and Joseph and Abraham, just to stick to one tribe,
all steered toward later tasks, like having a nationalized childhood.
But God and His messenger-angel have chosen a manchild of the wrong
        temperament—
Samson can't bear his divine assignment.
God and His angel have rushed too quickly to delegate a fate.
Then faults and limitations or even one's own civil war seem necessary,
rashness, imperfections, compelling, staring, half-beautiful in ways we
        can't understand,
and our drawbacks, blemishes, flaws re-surface, raised umbers long
        possessed,
like torso-birthmarks peered at, grazed by us, even cherished by another,
the way a thumb and pinkie compass the distance between moles on the
        beloved's body.

—*Richard J. Fein*

BAR MITZVAH BOY STUDIES THE LOBSTERS IN THE TANK

I wonder if they suffer,
their claws tied up like that—
like trying to yawn
with your elbows. Poor things,
I'd like to bust them out of there,
buy them up and let them all go
in the creek behind our house—
at $10.99 a pound,
and five dollars a week,
it would take me, let's see,
a pretty long time. That big one
climbing up on top of the others,
his foot in someone's eye—
what does it get him but closer
to the lobster pot? Better
to hide underneath or in back.
Be inconspicuous. Blend in.
Look out a window like
you're considering the weather—
tum-tee-tum. Even so,
they could call on you.
The world is like that.
But if you have the answer—
if you know your Torah portion
and your Haftarah portion
and all the songs and prayers—
you have nothing to fear. You can
sit anywhere. Hum a little tune.
Be conspicuous. Be idle. Be brazen.
When they call on you,
just start singing.
They'll praise you and maybe
give you enough money
to save all the lobsters—
which would be a real mitzvah.

—*Paul Hostovsky*

PIER REVIEW

Deep in the present rise the pilings
gone to rot beneath the pier.
They have upheld the past this long
with scarce a shred of scrutiny,
for nimble feet on the lovely old pier
proclaim it sound from year to year.
But oh, how the pilings grow weary.

Today, on the grand boards stretching out
a daring distance seaward, we see
the bishop gorgeously draped
in the colors and swash of his
festive engagement. We view as well
the hunch-backed fiddler, eager
to let rip, to loose the hundred-odd
dancers raring to reel. For starters

the bishop blesses the sea,
the old fishing fleet and fishermen,
even as he does each year.
Next, the fiddler strikes up
and the dancers begin to reel.

It starts as a bit of a wobble,
no hint of real trouble ahead,
till the reel ascends to thunder.

In not quite the blink of an eye
the pier goes down, and all upon it.

The new bishop is coming tomorrow.
A fiddler up from the boondocks
is rumored to bow the strings smartly.
The seven surviving reelers
have sworn to recruit a fresh order.

Pilings are coming from far away,
fine lumber for the walking planks.
The pier will jut a mile out,
abide no fears, and never rot.

It will host the bishop and fiddler
and reelers beyond number
for at least a thousand years.

—*Tomas O'Leary*

NATURAL HISTORY

I know the false description of evolution:
the slow march of amoeba to man

a sequence of progressing complexity.
Natural history is a pageant of disarticulation

punctuated by mass extinction. The universe's tendency
is towards collapse. In any case, grasp a fossil, a shadow

of it's past, take the nautilus, a chambered cephalopod.
We hold up the shell and try to show its growth

is relative to the moral development of man
Our work is small. We'll see what we want to see.

Forge a fortress out of a bombed out refuge
I don't know any other way but this—

After all, there's still art on the walls.

—*Teisha Dawn Twomey*

WHAT A POEM CAN DO TO YOU
*I can only read poetry when I'm strong
enough or destroyed enough.*
- Krista Tippet

If you open your heart to a poem, like a lover
opening his arms, and if the poem is written
in the poet's blood, you could be ravished.

Words can whisper sensuously in the shell
of your ear, like ocean ripples tickling
as you slowly submerge your head. Or they
can detonate inside your brain, a blinding
flash that reorders your senses.

If you are strong, the poet's words may thud
against your armor, dent your heart, send
vibrations deep into your body's core. But
if the words are perfectly chosen, precise,
they will slide like thin, sharp knives between
your ribs and finish you off, a sweet end to the pain.

—*Lawrence Kessenich*

ACOUSTIC LESSONS

How beautiful, I think, again,
standing in the guitar shop.

All these marvels of mahogany, rosewood,
spruce, sapele, maple, ebony, ash,

wild and sun-bound once, now kiln-dried,
planed, plied, curved, glued, clamped,

trussed, fretted, inlaid, lacquered,
tightly strung and precisely tuned

to feed our particular range of desire,
the varied rhythms and crooning blues of want

and regret and love and loneliness and exhilaration
and so on. I ask the clerk to take one down.

I sit on the worn stool, run my hand
up the back of the neck, admire

the complement of wood and wound steel,
press my fingers down against the strings,

strum one soft chord, let it resonate, feed the air,
fade away. Then another.

Minor, major, augmented, diminished.
It was twenty years ago that I put it all aside,

fingers sore and tired, my sad-sack heart hammered
by the knowledge of what it would take to really know.

In my sorry head, Mississippi John Hurt sings,
voice half gone, but more sure of itself than ever:

Cheer up my brother, live in the sunshine.
We'll understand it all by and by.

                                        —*Michael Brosnan*

DON'T EXPLAIN

Written as a protest
poem Billie Holiday prays
with eyes closed

for the lynching to end
as piano keys remember
the impossible,

a father, who abandoned her
as an infant, and the 1930 incident
in Marion, Indiana,

a mob of white men break
into the city jail using sledge-
hammers; they beat

and hang two black
suspects from nearby poplar
trees: "Here is a fruit

for the crows to pluck / For
the rain to gather, for the wind to
suck / For the sun to rot,

for the tree to drop / Here
is a strange and bitter crop,"
young Billie Holiday's

slow, bluesy jazz crushes
the ginned, cigarette choked
room at Café Society,

Greenwich Village chic,
where waiters stop all service
for the *scent of magnolias.*

—*Gary Rainford*

THE MERRY-GO-ROUND

"Here comes the Hobo!" someone said.
It was a hungry looking clown
who wore a give-me-something frown,
his nose a stewed tomato red,
his painted lips, blood sausage brown.

Then clouds were whirling round a sky
some giant used a tree to stir.
My parents' faces all a blur,
I kept on waving them goodbye
not really knowing where they were.

"Stop!" my father hollered. "Sir!"
On every face behind a smudge
of caramel or melted fudge
two eyes bugged out. "Get off of her!"
The slumped-back hobo didn't budge.

My father dragged him off the ride
growling that he'd break his teeth.
My little sister couldn't breathe.
Those kids all took the hobo's side
against the girl trapped underneath.

—*Alfred Nicol*

STUCK IN A TRAFFIC JAM NEAR
VICTORIA'S TERMINAL IN BOMBAY

I sit in the backseat with my mother while
the driver traces the voices from the radio.
two filthy hands
slap the newly cleaned glass
of my window. Mama tells me
not to look
but the rhythm of their banging
makes me cave in. I am
not surprised by little naked children,
white flakes
of dried snot smeared on their chapped faces.
or maybe it is drugs.
I've seen far too many children, necks hanging
on the nooses of addiction
controlled by underground mafias—far too many to hope
that maybe they are different.
but they're all the same. They
carry little white plastic bags
with glue to sniff on, their eyes
are droopy and they beg
spitting out white froth and occasional words.instead of money,
this time I give them sandwiches I had saved for later
they snatch them away
from me while calling me a selfish prostitute in hindi.
running away to a corner, they hand it to a man who
smacks them on their heads.
I see the boy's tears and helplessness
and in that moment I regret and wonder,
maybe I should've just given them the 10 rupee note instead.

—*Simrin Tamhane*

A CALCULATED RISK

Dad down-shifts the Civic just before the intersection.
He thinks he's lucky the light is green.
His wife chatters about the graduation.
Their only daughter, the valedictorian,
sits behind mom, seatbelt snug. Dad
hears the sirens, catches the blue light
in the corner of his eye, the cruiser
coming on fast like a low flying jet.
He thinks, What? Hits the gas to get
out of the way, but the cruiser
hammers the Honda's rear passenger door,
crumpling the metal, fracturing the window,
the frame closing in on the daughter
like a metal claw, indifferent
to her screams, her flawless skin,
her taut muscles from years of dance,
her youth, her beautiful blue eyes.

Dad blames himself for not seeing the cruiser sooner.
Mom blames the kid the cops were chasing,
the one who got away in the stolen car.
We all know there is no one to blame.

She is lucky to survive, the doctors say.
Three months later she sits
in the wheelchair ready to go home.
She has full use of her left hand
and partial vision in her left eye.
She is optimistic about the future.

—*Ed Meek*

BLUE, CERULEAN BLUE

Blue, cerulean blue
sapphire and turquoise
azure and lapis lazuli
as vast as the sea
the untouchable sky
endlessly deep
too far to see.

When you were with me
it was apricot sunrise
mango, and petals of rose
sweet strawberries,
pomegranate and peony
hibiscus and peach
blushing buds of an apple tree
blossoms bending for me to reach.

Then you were gone
and the nectarine dawn
was shrouded
in shadow and clouds,
gray-

blue,

cyan and peacock
cobalt and china blue
teal and viridian:
They beckon me
to an ocean of indigo
to a midnight blue
where the sky meets the sea.

Blue

will pull me and carry me
to a distant horizon,
a coral island.
I will ride
on the cresting waves, as the tide
sweeps me up in its hands
'til it sets me to rest
on the pink, pearly sand.

I'll stand
while wavelets lap at my feet

aquamarine
tinged with tangerine.

And all alone
in a copper sunset
I'll drop
a colorless tear
in an ocean of
blue.

—*Lucy Holstedt*

ASTONISHMENT

When it arrives, it's more likely
to seem a sparrow bedraggled by
three days of rain than some
day-glo lightning bolt, a wild
underhang of feathers
below its tricolor brown, black
and white. Until you notice
it's way too hefty, the beak is
pink and wrong, and that's not
the sparrow's grab-and-go at
the feeder: it is hanging around
as if lost, a blow-in on a northeast
storm who has followed the locals
to a seed source, its white eyestripe
and lunula at first perhaps
a Sam Peabody bird's, only then
the astonishment that it may be
from Thule or Flatey. Though it
matches up with photos
of stragglers to the Aleutians
and Orkneys, there's been
no sighting of its kind here ever.
Ordinary where it lives, for an hour
it's a godsend from the marvelous,
not for anyone caught in
a type-A lifelist competition.

—*Brendan Galvin*

SUPPER

We lounge on the lawn,
Alice and I,
in Adirondack
chairs and shorts
and I have gone
shirtless this evening
in mid-summer,
the sun hanging
behind a screen
of trees, one branch-
less, scarred and scorched
from when the tool shed
was torched years ago—
lounge in the graying,
motionless, air
mosquitoes adore,
moaning, ravening
for your blood,
swarming, keening
to land and score
the crucial meal
to ensure, by feeding
their larvae, survival
of their carnal species,
we're meanwhile
into baguette and paté,
fromage and tangelo,
as here and there
around us dragonflies,
long-bodied, black—
swoop! streak! swerve!
an air armada!
a flying flotilla!
they cruise and patrol,
protect and serve
and more than help
defend and keep us
safe! snap! gulp!

Golly.

—*Llyn Clague*

SALISBURY SUMMER

Summer on Salisbury Beach,
a week at my Aunt's cottage,
adults worked all day,
Two cousins and I left on our own.
At ten years old unfamiliar,
but desired, days of freedom.
Instructions: "You can go to
the beach but stay near lifeguards."
Our unknowing babysitters,
who paid little attention,
more focused on bathing beauties,
applying sunscreen, on blankets nearby.
We rode waves so rough
they slammed us into the strand,
filled our bathing suits with sand.
We arose coughing and sputtering
from swallowed salt water
then raced through the surf
to catch another wild ride.
When bored, we walked
to jetty of large, black rocks,
lept from boulder to boulder,
scraped hands and feet
on slippery, rough surfaces,
while sea pounded through
gaps in rock pile below.
In evening we would wander home,
fall asleep early with expectations
for another day that
would be fully ours.

—*Lainie Senechal*

DOWN

Each season now, their numbers in free fall,
titmouse, nut-hatch groundward sink, like leaves hushed,
dislodged by a tickling breeze. Featherweight
ounces downed: rot, duff, soil.

At a pond's edge: flecks, shadows as wings lost
past eyesight drift, spied late in sunlight—molt
as leaves blown to shirred ripples, against shore
or dam-grate perched to hush.

Razzmatazz of chain saws:
bite and grind, heartwood gnawed, eaten. Airwaves
nearby shatter, go numb.

How can you expect the birds
to sing when their groves are cut down?

(Thoreau: his sentence, before the clear cuts,
before skies black with passenger pigeons
emptied out, his judgment

on men who sawed by hand, heard the axe-heads
lodge *ch-thuk*, into pith,
yanked the haft loose for the next muscling strokes.)

Toothed blades sing out their burden: elegies
for silence, leaf-homes downed. Who expects speech-
less deafened birds to breed?

—Daniel A. Harris

O WOMAN GET OFF THE ROCK

O woman get off the rock   take your thumbs off your keypad
bring both feet into March   clear your rheumy eyes
four white-tails ogle you so close you can smell
their wild   you're breathing in their steamy billows
wake up   turn off your this and that   winter's last dark
tongue is quiet   there's froth and spray from the mallards' startle
the mucky river's cascading   the bog's a ruckus you've never heard
before   listen   redwings trill away for love and power
three hawks keeeeeee arr in dives for chipmunks   trees anticipate
their leaves and offer up their tenancies   the only ice patch left
on the trail disappears with a whimper   woman   pay attention
that poem in your head   the one about the brother dying
family full of shame may well be written   or not   dry
prairie grass zithers a tune   milk weeds clack their pod drums
and streams plash and splish   a gust cyclones an oak leaf pile
unplug yourself girl   the prairie writes the poem now and
now as it did yesterday and the day before and will long after
your body's a tree and your vapors seed the clouds

—*Susan Nisenbaum Becker*

INTERVIEW WITH PULITZER-PRIZE-WINNING
NOVELIST PAUL HARDING

Interviewed by Nicole Cadro

Endicott College had the pleasure of hosting 2010 Pulitzer Prize- winning novelist Paul Harding on April 7, 2016. He was a speaker in the Endicott College/Ibbetson Street Press Visiting Author Series. His prize-winning novel *Tinkers* deals with a dying father and a son who returns to tend to him. Laura Miller, who was on the selection committee for the Prize wrote, " I think, sentence for sentence, it was the most beautifully written and had the most gorgeous use of language of any books that we looked at." At the event, Harding captured the audience's attention as soon as he uttered the first words. His poetic prose had a rhythm that kept listeners buckled into the roller coaster of words that came together to create this lyrical literary piece. It was a distinct pleasure to have a conversation with an individual as engaging as Paul Harding.

Nicole Cadro: I read that Carlos Fuentes' *Terra Nostra* was the work that you read that flipped the switch and helped you decide you wanted to become a writer. I was hoping you could elaborate on that, what specifically about that work made up your mind?

Paul Harding: When I read that book it was a time in my life that I was an avid reader, but my own reading was not self-directed very well. I had not found the kind of books that I wanted to read. So I was reading other books, the ones I read in college, but I knew somewhere there was the headwaters or the writing that I could really dig into and relate to. So, actually, the most intuitive thing that I would do is just go into the fiction section of the local bookstore, in Amherst or wherever (I went to UMass Amherst), and I would look for the thickest books I could find that weren't just "pop" novels. I would just pull them off the shelf and look at them; that's how I ended up reading Thomas Mann and Tolstoy, and I just found *Terra Nostra* because *Terra Nostra* is just like a brick, like a doorstop. And I thought, "I want me some of that." That is what I want to do.

First of all, I want to be in conversation with works of art that are that large in scale. I write actually quite small books but I think of them as being really dense, they are one hundred and fifty pages long but hopefully they are seven hundred and fifty pages sort of dense. Just that vision and just the fact, the license he had, I didn't know you could do that. You get to write about all of this wild stuff and his vocabulary was really exotic and esoteric. It's funny, because I don't write like him at all, or not so much anymore. In subsequent years, I am almost afraid to go back and read that again because I don't think I'd like it as much. It just set me off on that trajectory. It was one of those funny things, the old version of that book had an afterword by the novelist Milan Kundera; he wrote *The Unbearable Lightness of Being* and I read that, and then I read some of Fuentes' essays and he talked about how much he loved Thomas Mann. So, then, from that one book and just that one author I started finding all of these other authors—until now it's hopeless. But I take comfort in that: I'll never be able to read all of the books I want to read, it will never run out.

Cadro: To branch off of that question, what about once you started to delve into your literary career and your schooling, specifically college. I know that I look for things to take away from every class. I think, "Okay this might help me later on in life." What was a big thing in your schooling that you feel really affected your career and your path?

Harding: Well, undergraduate was a little bit of this and that. I was an English major, so I kind of cut my teeth and worked up my chops by reading a lot of Shakespeare and similar works, which I spend a lot of my time doing now, too. But, sort of circumstantially, all the while I was in college I played drums in rock bands and that's what I ended up doing ten years after that. So I was thinking about music a lot, but also thinking of it as art. A lot of it was and it just so happened that UMass Amherst had a really good AfroAm (African American) department and studies program, and at the time I was there they had really amazing Jazz musicians there, too. So, I was able to listen to lectures about art and about music by people like Max Roach, a very famous Jazz drummer. I was able to take a yearlong course called Revolutionary Concepts in African American Music with a Jazz sax player named Archie Shepp, who was just a really extraordinary guy. I found that all of the guys I hung out with were these pretty radical music dudes from New York City. I had grown up in Wenham, Massachusetts, and then I had these new, informative experiences about art, but also about social justice and race in America, and art forms that arose out of that in the black community. It really furnished a context for thinking about art for the rest of my life that has never changed. I still feel that initial thing and that is what is still evolving.

Cadro: Our English 101 class just had a guest speaker, Robin Stratton, and she talked a lot more about the writing process itself versus the actual works. When you were writing *Tinkers* was there page ripping, fingernails flying frustration? Then, if there was this frustration, how did you know you had "it"?

Harding: That's a good question because with me it's very intuitive. I don't write things in a linear way. I sort of collage. I have all sorts of weird, mixed metaphors that I use, so I sort of think of it as a big painting. I add layer after layer, then scrape layers off and add more layers, and just sort of collage and move things all around, very improvisational and musical. All I can report was that there was one day when I finished writing whatever the passage was that I was working on, and I sat back and I realized, "I've got the whole thing, the whole thing's here. I've told the story." But then I had to go back and put it all in order, because I had written it in such a crazy way, sort of a mess.

Cadro: So it was kind of like putting all of the pieces into the timeline?

Harding: Yeah, basically, more or less it was doing it chronologically. But in *Tinkers* the point of view is a guy who is in his final illness and his consciousness is starting to dissipate. It's just the way his memory works and doesn't work, and the way the ideas surface and then sink back down and then recrudesce in weird refracted ways. So, I had to fool around with that and get it so it was almost prismatic; I had to make it a cohesive whole. But, chronologically, what I did was I printed it up and I cut the whole manuscript up into all the different scenes and pieces. I put them all out on the floor and I spent a weekend rearranging them into the prism. The published novel is forty-thousand words and the original manuscript was probably about seventy-thousand words, so I cut about a third of it. There is not a sentence in that book that I didn't rewrite thirty times.

Cadro: How long did it take you?

Harding: It took me probably four years to write it, to really get to the point where I felt I could show it and try to get it published. But, then, nobody would publish it; so I had it on my hands for another five years. Once in a while I would take it out on a Sunday or Saturday night and just fiddle around with it and just keep trying to get the language as precise and lucid as I could make it.

Cadro: I bet those publishers are kicking themselves now.

Harding: (*Chuckles*) There are a few who wrote me nasty rejection letters, and when it won the Prize, I thought, "Told you."

Cadro: So, my last question for you is a two-part question. *Tinkers*, I know, is mainly focused on a man dying and going through all of those ideas and memories. He's kind of facing, reflecting on, his life and also facing death; you must have had to ponder a lot of that on your own. So, what do you strive to take out of each day?

Harding: That's a good question, because I don't approach each day with the idea that there has to be a "take away" from it. It's to be observant; it's just that idea of being as fully engaged and conscious and aware as possible. It's inextricable because I'm always thinking in the context of writing. I think of my writing as having no lessons to be had; my writing is experiential, it's descriptive, so what I mean to do is make my prose. Whatever I'm working on, I have something of the density of lived experience, so when other people read it there will be recognition, they'll recognize.

Cadro: So, every day is an experience, adding on to what could come out of your literature?

Harding: Yeah, yeah. Then I mean there's always—because I'm preoccupied with theology and I read tons of philosophy—I'm always thinking about morality and ethics and just "loving your neighbor" and all of that sort of stuff. So often, the "takeaway" is that I'll try to do better tomorrow. It's sort of like falling short of your own ideal, just being mindful in that way and trying to be honest. As a writer, one of the principle things is that everything you write needs to be true.

Cadro: The second part of that question was you also deeply explored the possibility of death; do you think this made you more comfortable with death?

Harding: I don't know…you know, it's funny, I don't think of it as death, I think of the subject as mortality. Because that's philosophy and religion and all of that sort of stuff. Artistically and aesthetically, too, it's kind of the ultimate counterpoint. It's the ultimate juxtaposition, it sets in relief being, the whole idea of nonbeing or the whole idea of why is there something instead of nothing—metaphysics. Because, just by disposition, I spend a lot of time thinking about metaphysics and consciousness and the nature of consciousness, and out of what does consciousness precipitate? Some substratum? Or is it a function of complexity, like biological, something that gets complicated enough so it's an emergent property. It's a great mystery. A lot of times, too, I just get cranky because popular writers—like celebrity science writers or celebrity philosophers—give people a portrait of the human mind and of human life that is so impossibly simplistic and simple-minded that it just makes me crazy. They explain everything away, and really it's rhetorical, just slight of hand with grammar, language games. Partly, I just think of it as my, (and again this is an idea), but just that if art stands for anything it stands for a corrective against simplifying human experience, taking away the dignity of each person's human experience by presuming to tell people what it is that their lives, in fact, consist of, because it's been empirically demonstrated by some positive-esque "jerk-off." Just that idea that what your art does is that it bears true witness to the experience of life—and that's the key, because if there is that authenticity and you can get that authenticity on the page that's the deepest connection you can make with the reader, which is that the reader will recognize herself in your art. Very humanistic, very old school humanism.

MYCENAE REVISITED

1.
He kept going back to the phrase, "inside the wall,"
Convinced that a cryptic passage in Pausanias
Led to the beehive tombs, preserved in amber—

If Heinrich Schliemann understood the grammar.
Glory congealed. Kleos bright as the disk
Of the sun god, Ra. The mask of Agamemnon...

And was it a fluke, or an omen, the text came roughly
Seventeen-hundred years after the fall of Troy,
And here he was, consulting it as his guide,

Seventeen-hundred years later? From gaps in the text
He tapped dark sleep for the glint of gilded dream-vessels,
Heard loose millennial sediment sifted through shovels

Sunk into vaguely oracular, vast lacunae.

2.
An hour from Argos, my uncle Taki's cellar.
Or bunker. Damp clay floors and hurricane lamp.
The gleam of grapes in open bins. And dark

Red Mavrodaphne circulating through tubes
Of a homemade still. Ensconced on crates, we toasted
The *kéfalotíri*: those thick rank heads of cheese

Above our heads, their goat's milk cured by hanging
From the rafters. My uncle called them The Colonels.
The breathing, earthen walls of the Peloponnese

Were porous and moist. The cheese suspended by strings.
Out of the deep dank cellar dark of a dream
They come floating back, like disembodied chunks

Of hacked-up marble. Never far from Argos.

3.
Trenches cut at the close of the nineteenth century.
Scaffolds propped at steep angles. The site gouged out.
Inside the wall. Go back to an earlier entry.

Read it again. Bear down on the relevant terms.
Inside the word for *wall* the sound of *fate.*
Teixei implied in *teixoi*. Burial chambers

As echo chambers. Pore over *péribóli*,
The circular border enclosing a sanctuary.
Under a sandy hill, parabolic passages.

The convoluted plots and unsettled ashes
Turning over like syntax in an hour glass.
Inside the wall. Beneath the earth. That burnished

Threshold where staunch Orestes unsheathed his blade.

4.
In the famous photograph of Schliemann's Greek bride,
She's wearing the jeweled headdress, necklace and earrings:
Adornments from Troy: Sophia at Seventeen.

—*George Kalogeris*

JAMES WRIGHT'S HAMMOCK

Empty,
It rocks slightly
In the imperceptible mid-summer breeze,
The once white rope bronzed by sun and rain, frayed.
Midday rays slowly scorch
The tall grass gone to seed,
A pair of silent scrub pines
Re-measuring seven gray field stones
Between them. Fence post remnants
Slide into the ravine.
From a dusty corner nest
In the Duffy's abandoned barn,
A swallow swoops its sickle-like wings,
Snatches a butterfly in flight,
Orange disappearing
as quickly as it arrived.
This is where the dream drifts toward dawn.

—*Tom Laughlin*

PUNCTUATION

In this story
you are the Capital letter
and I, a semi-colon;
separating two independent
but related clauses.

We tell of our first meeting
among words, in the bookstore,
a cool November sun
slanting shafts of light
through glass doors, shimmering
on the skins of books,
histories of other lives.

I felt the heft of you
reading over my shoulder --
Marcel Proust— "Swann's Way"—

like a blue heron's feathery wings,
your arms brushed over my hair;

I turned to find your eyes,
the color of moist earth.

The book is here on our desk,
its cover, once the glossy bronze
of an autumn glade,
now faded to a burnt blonde.

We pause, a caesura,
honor the space between words,
in the lines of our lives

and speak of how we met,
and met again, in years
of dizzying spirals,
all leading to this moment.

That night,
when you told me your story,
I reached across the space
between strangers,
to enfold you—

I, a bracket
and you, an ellipsis...

—*Ruth Chad*

NO EXPECTATIONS

I packed a few things,
a book of new poems,

tucked away, with my sandals
and shirt for our day.
What to expect?
Imagined possibilities rise
from long abandoned hopes
like bubbles in Perrier.

No expectations
you said.

I'll take the boat
across the bay—
will you be waiting
when I come in?

It's been ten years
since we parted,
you going to Africa.
The gouda cheese I bought—
will it be enough for lunch?
Or will we have a glass of wine?

Just walk around
you said.

I don't know what you'll think
my hair gone frizzy gray.
So much I could say,
but here I am.

The boat fare
six dollars.
It's too much
for such a short way.
I should swim
the entire mile,
emerge like a seal,
sleek—and smile
at your surprise.

(*continued*)

Did you remember
that today I would come?
Will you still be so tall and thin
waiting at the top of the gangway?

It's only me
with my faded Bosox hat
and crinkly toes.
How long is it
since we dug in the low tide slime
and listened to the seashells hum?

And you
dripped castles of mud,
threw sand in my hair;
your laughter sparkled in the air
while the sea wiped bare
our imagination's grandest designs.

Will you smile and wave
when the boat comes in
and the captain throws the line.

I'll be the first off
if I can.

No expectations.

—*Sandra Thaxter*

IN KENSINGTON GARDENS THAT DAY

Fiona was first to spot one,
perhaps because
she was smallest, closest to the ground.

We all scurried over quickly, bent down, and
soon, we, too, could see them.
They were why we had come
to Kensington Gardens that day.
We could scarcely contain our joy.

Fiona had heard them singing
in thickets along the Serpentine, too.
As dusk drew longer, darker
we felt the air tingling with activity
buzzing with preparations.

Tiny sounds emanated from beneath
huge old Spanish chestnut trees.
Soon it would be time for the little folk
to dance on the lawns.
After dark, after the big people had gone.

Eager to share in our joy,
a woman passing by
in her navy blue business suit
followed us to the old chestnuts.

She searched beneath each tree,
scanned little caverns between heavy roots,
appeared puzzled, dismayed, lost.
Dismissing us, she stood up, walked on.
She had not seen the fairies.

But there was great joy for us
in Kensington Gardens that day
for there, beneath the roots
of ancient chestnut trees
we had found the fairies
right where we knew
they would be.

—*Babara Claire Kasselmann*

MORTALS WITH SPIRITS

An E-vite landed in my e-mail from cyberspace.
My first fleeting thought was to delete it.
Unknown address suggested spam;
Perhaps a virus- Heaven forbid!

Morbid curiosity deposed the discreet.
Opened, concern turned to amazement.
The content stated, in a short announcement:
"We regret to advise you that Time Passed away.
A wake is scheduled at Chapel of the Stars.
All sentiments are welcome."

No hour offered, just a date and directions
To a mesa in New Mexico; and a promise
Of a spirited event.
I don't know when I assented; but, arriving
There, I found standing room only—
Not even a seat in sight.

Attired in white linen finery,
Time reposed in open coffin.
His shorn locks were at an
Orderly shoulder length;
Former copious beard,
Scythed to a mere van dyke.

His visage evoked dried figs.
We stood still, silenced, stunned.
All had believed the myth
That Time was, well, timeless;
But there he was, serenely asleep.

We recalled the sundry junctures
When It was taken for granted.
In our youth, we little noted its flow,
Though we had boated daily on the river.
Now, all seemed beyond retrieval.

We uncorked a few bottles, perhaps more
Than a few, which we consumed
Yes, in no time at all.
The throngs were in fine spirits.
We were ebullient.
Our eyes absorbed the stars.

We celebrated, swapped memories,
Resuscitated some long submerged.
The imbibing continued unabated.
A last bottle was decisively passed around.
Sound was sagely mitigated.
We paid our somber respects
To departed Time.

Nothing left to do but to drift
Back to our separate parts,
Known and not, somewhat sober –
Well, still a bit drunk, if you must know.
Bereft, tottering, we suffered Time to pass.

—*Harris Gardner*

HEART OF STONE

We were kids, my heart
on a sleeve
yours a stone
you would not share
anything personal
I should have known then
months of waste
imagination could have
known excitement, joy
in those empty days
you like a ball bouncing
away to another wall
or field
while I on the front porch
whittled a piece of wood
into a dog

—*Zvi A . Sesling*

THE FIGURE

Look: there again, haunting the shaggy fringe of
delirium dreams is the shabby specter
walking encumbered, encrusted, left
as always stranded by the receding tide of

florescent night, hermit sheltered in the
large cast-off down parka shell, cold spring
wind blowing him along this recurring stretch
of city street, with forgotten newspaper

headlines and stories folded within, becoming
part of his personal history, integrating,
disintegrating into this being
of complex resolve—buffeted, baffling
resilience on display, one-man parade seeming,
oddly enough, largely invisible.

His wheeled grey upright cart, too, holds up, holding
string-tied findings and whatever remains of
Before. Curling grey-bristle whiskers and hair cling
to an ageless ghost-face, plastered like sea plants

waiting for the pocked moon revolving to
bring back a wash of breathable ocean.
With sunken eyes looking like their round blackness
belongs on hard-shell stalks, next to feelers
waving in some green-hued plastic tank,

you may imagine he is waiting for the
final deluge or boiling apocalypse,
or that he has—improbably, against
all odds—lived through such things, and

now returned, bearing his burden of witness
beyond words and symbols, the only survivor.

—Kirk Etherton

TRIPLE-ARCH BRIDGE

Frank Bolles passed here in sunrise
on a walk to Blue Hill, winter eighteen-ninety.
He recorded *the pretty triple-arch bridge*
over the Neponset. Snow fleas
beguiled him, though the view was *injured*
by the smoke of Boston from cellars of coal.

I've plodded that Quincy granite span
twenty-three years. Paul's Bridge.
I fancied it a saunter, seated half-lotus
with neighborhood muffin and coffee,
twenty minutes of riverbank watch
before hauled back on my feet,
up-street to the college. Puzzling
Paul who? Who Paul?

Then Dunkin' Donuts squatted a derelict
gas station, knocked out the local
donut and lunch place. Nothing
museful then, toting Dunkie's
Neponset-side. Pneumonia
culled Bolles at thirty-eight. I tramp
across Paul's at sixty, a glance
at the water for heron or ducks.

Didn't used to see wild turkeys
in those river-watch years,
ganged, possed, or raftered
as they are now, across the lawns
up Brush Hill Road. The birds refrain
from attacking this foot commuter,
so far. Though a hurtling deer
nearly bowled me over.

For Bolles, snow fleas. Now turkeys
and deer spill from Blue Hill
to here. Sixty-four deer
taken out in a December cull.
"I was the lucky first one"
said the first man to topple a legal doe
since Frank Bolles ended his
thigh-deep tramping through
Land of the Lingering Snow.

—David Miller

THE LONGFELLOW

Unrecognizable, its towers down;
passage and portal still, but much reduced—
the Red Line's fine view of the Charles is screened;
crowds press down the one side open to use.

The span's named for a poet laureate—
the products, both, of previous centuries.
The poet's dead, the bridge deteriorates;
under repairs which stretch eternally.

Structural steel, each huge piece custom-made,
cannot be fitted to the aging frame;
each section here has settled, warped with age.
Better demolish it, and start again?

Each day that I traverse it, as I must,
its ornamental iron flakes off in rust.

—*Denise Provost*

METFERN CEMETERY

In a meadow bounded by fieldstone, space
opening suddenly to sky on a forested trail,
a large sign announces: "From 1947 to 1979
about 310 burials," the exact number
apparently unknown.

Cement blocks mark the graves: P for Protestant,
C for Catholic, beside numbers where you expect
names: long-time inmates, disabled or poor,
from state institutions closed years ago.

The pedestal of a statue is all that remains
of a memorial, now covered with grimy plastic lilies,
a bunch of dried asters, a small bust of Jesus—
robe open to reveal his sacred heart—as if he alone
could love them.

—*Ruth Smullin*

QUIXOTE COUNTRY

Hours of flat brown landscape
a boy across the aisle whining
quiero agua quiero agua

donde mi paquete donde mi paquete
until abuelita threatens basta
o sopapo and the boy winces

expecting a slap sneezes
as the train tilts into a curve and
grimy windows frame la vieja

hunched in black lifting
her rake to shout curses at us
shaking her fist at the iron

monster spitting smoke
staining earth and sky
coughing insults on her garden

the train crawls through country
arid enough for dragons
and phantom windmills

anything to fill this void
scanning desert I see
Sancho on a dusty mule

Don Q clanking in armor
lifting his lance as he spurs
noble nag Rocinante.

—*Nina Rubenstein Alonso*

Translations:
line 3: I want water I want water
line 4: where's my package, where's my package
line 5: grandmother (abuelita) enough (basta)
line 6: or a slap (sopapo)

WHEN MILTON FLEW THE COOP*

when I consider how my light is spent
e're half my days, in this bottle pent,
and that one talent which is flight or hide
keeps me fearful, though my quest's
more bent to serve therewith the unknown,
and circumvent the inner confines of self doubt,
and chide the philosopher's confounding aside.

I would decide to flea and fly if I could,
to which the propounder replies, he does not need
me inside or out. he seeks to play with the gravity
of the bottle with and without.

I serve him best, his trait of sparkling insights,
each making bright my fate, by giving lift
to what might be less, to alight or to rest:
they also serve who, when in flight, have no weight.

—*Peter Fulton*

*John Milton's response to Ludwig Wittgenstein's
challenge: "to shew the fly the way out of the fly-bottle."

THE ANVIL CLOUD

For Chris Mann

I came up out of Kansas I came
       russet rain
          drought then thunderstorm
out of the plains
over the great plains
burnt-umber bluestem
burnt-sienna buffalo grass
ivory-black
       ivory-white cumulonimbus
from Iowa to Oklahoma
       out of the whirlwind
came hail
and rain.
       All the farmer said was:

"Weather sure is good for the corn!
But Goddamn it's a ruinin' the beans."

—Wendell Smith

BE WELL,

says the checkout clerk at Walgreens.
I'm fourth in line.
Are those tears welling in his eyes?

He sneezes a messy sneeze.
The ponytailed woman sniffs, taking her bagged Purell from his hand.

An old man's next, buys a styrofoam cup of dehydrated soup.
Be well.
The man gurgles, *Well, hell,* and hobbles away.

A child is screaming.
Her mother wrenches a Snickers bar from her hand.
Be well, he offers, but they're on a forced march to the door.

Now it's my turn.
I place my box of bandaids on the counter
and bow my head, await his blessing.

—Mary Buchinger

MISERERE

Agnus mundi,
qui tollis peccata
populi,
miserere nobis.
For the covenant
shredded again
in willful neglect,
miserere nobis.
For the melting of glaciers
and the loss of chrystal
ruggedness, *miserere nobis.*
For the rising of sea levels,
marshes drunk on tidal swell,
miserere nobis.
For the decay of coral reefs,
the stripping of land,
the beheading of mountains,
Miserere.

For denuding forests, Miserere.
For the fate of Tuvalu, Miserere.
For drought draining
tributaries of the Amazon, Miserere.

For the meltdown at Fukishima, *miserere nobis.*

A continent of trash
drifts in the North Pacific
awaiting forgiveness.

Polar bears marooned
on ice floes await mercy.

Have compassion on the cod,
the mackerel, pollock and flounder.

Bless the lobster,
shrimp and crab—
they have not sinned.

Comfort the refugees
of our greed and waste.
Provide for their needs.
Lead them out
of their desert states.

For the thinning of tuna
and the wasting of whales,
miserere.
For the dolphin slaughter
at Kaiji, *miserere,*
and land melt in Tuk,
miserere.

For dimming the kingfisher's fire
and the dragonflies' flame, *miserere nobis.*

Before the dearest freshness
deep down things disappear,
dona nobis ah! spem

—T. Michael Sullivan

Author's Note: The Agnus Dei is a prayer in the Latin
Mass that asks for mercy and concludes with a plea
for peace. I have altered it slightly to reflect the
circumstances. Also, "spem" means "hope."

FOR JOHN WILLIAMS

Every time I entered
the office for a conference
with you, my graduate school adviser,
I turned clumsy. Dropped a book
my shoes treated like a soccer ball.
Or fumbled through our text's five sections
while the poem I wanted to ask you about
stayed hidden on some other page.

Worse, when we discussed the poems
I'd labored over till near dawn
for your Creative Writing course,
your scrutiny, spotlight bright, showed me
why the stanzas I had thought I turned
into swans were still ugly ducklings.

      Now, a surge of sadness
flows through my body. Aided
by the advice from you
I gradually absorbed and applied,
whatever poems of worth I've written
were, like belated messages,
crafted only after the last time
that you turned off the office light
and darkness took your eyes.

—Robert K. Johnson

TOP OFF

I can sit on summer days in just my preschool panties
topless with the boys until mother says I should cover up
While my brother stays bare breasted at the table
and father parades a push mower self-powered in browning nipples
Mother wears a full cup for complete coverage
that straps-in deep leaving red ridges pinching it all closed
Tight the way my khakis cut-crease in the crotch stinging
from the dig of chino fabric that mother feels fit me just fine
At nine I notice breasts grow as cone-shaped bulges
from the fronts of girls who don't seem to mind but mine
Tout tiny in itchy knots and my nipples puff like pig skin popcorn
so I punch them black and blue to make them flat
The perky-thorax girls prod my back for a strap
that isn't there and mother tells all the cousins at Christmas
Who laugh into the ketchuped shrimp and I run home
murmuring boobs boobs boobs after watching a farm film on
Dairy cows overflowing their udders attached to milking machines
and even the pediatrician has me waiting topless on his table
Lying stripped as an almost-ripe plum for his hot-lick hands
pushing hard enough to leave a thumb spot and peeking down my panties
As mother glorifies a full length open bottomed girdle
snug and strangled by six garters insisting it feels good
All the while poking to pester the shape of my breasts as though they're
poor-box vagrants sleeping on pizza board in need of a more permanent home

—*Lisa D. Kaufman*

THE BEES

Part I.

I'm scared of Bees
Swarming around
All the sweet things
Look to hide themselves

Swarming around
Squeezing into these tight spaces
Look to hide themselves
Sneaking in, under doorways, through cracks
                    -Broken window screens

Squeezing into these tight spaces
I hear them buzzing
Sneaking in under doorways, through cracks
                    -Broken window screens
Talking to each other

I hear them buzzing
about the work, this attack
Talking to each other
See, how fragile and small I am

About the work, this attack
All the sweet things
See how fragile and small I am
I'm scared of bees

Part II.

In the corner of something
Our room, a doorway, my mind
A long proboscis drains sweet nectar
Translucent, paper wings

Our room, a doorway, my mind
Fear is waiting, or trying to blend into
Translucent, paper wings
These huge crushing fists
Fear is waiting or trying to blend into
The sting, pheromone, sound the alarm
These huge crushing fists
Segmented body-three parts of sting

The sting, pheromone, sound the alarm
Nothing hurts after the first prick
Segmented body -three parts of sting
Mouth, Hands, Body

Nothing hurts after the first prick
all the sweet things
Mouth, Hands, Body
I'm scared of bees

—Susan LaFortune

THE ENVY OF THE GODS

Because we feared the envy of the gods
We hid the love we felt. We strived, inspired
By days and weeks of breaking up old sods
To live like farmers, overworked and tired.

We bought a house that no one else would want.
Aware our cash would never add a speck
To books that measure wealth, we did not taunt
Our luck but cashed and hoarded every check.

We filled our plot with modest herbs and greens.
Beneath the burning sun, the falling star,
We spit on passion, acted out in scenes
To trick the gods observing from afar

That they might praise what we had undertaken:
A quiet life, hardworking and soft-spoken.

—Joyce Wilson

Nina Rubinstein Alonso's poetry has appeared in *Ploughshares, The New Yorker, Bagel Bards, Ibbetson Street, The New Boston Review, MomEgg, U. Mass. Review*, etc., and her stories in *Southern Women's Review*, one a Pushcart nominee, and *Broadkill Review*. David Godine Press published her book *This Body*. She works with *Constellations*: A Journal of Poetry and Fiction (www.constellations-lit.com) and directs Fresh Pond Ballet School in Cambridge, Massachusetts (www.freshpondballet.com).

Jennifer Barber teaches at Suffolk University in Boston, where she is founding and current editor of the literary journal *Salamander*. Her poems have appeared widely in magazines and journals, including the *New Yorker*, the *Missouri Review, Poetry, Post Road, upstreet, Poetry Daily*, and the *Gettysburg Review*. Her poetry collections are *Works on Paper*, which received the 2015 Tenth Gate Prize (The Word Works, 2106), and *Given Away* and *Rigging the Wind*, both from Kore Press (2012, 2003).

Susan Nisenbaum Becker is a psychotherapist, poet, actor, playwright and collaborative performer with musicians and dancers, reading and performing locally, nationally and internationally. Her work is forthcoming or published in the *Harvard Review, Salamander, Lumina, Calyx*, and *Poetry East*, among other magazines. She's received numerous awards including residencies at Yaddo, MacDowell, Ragdale and the Virginia Center for the Creative Arts.

Molly Mattfield Bennett has published in several magazines including *Knock, Antioch* (Seattle), *Ibbetson Street, Constellations* and *Off the Coast*. In 2010, *Name the Glory* was published by Wilderness House Press, and in June 2012 she read at the Jeff Male Memorial Reading at the William Joiner Institutes' Writers Conference at the University of Massachusetts Boston. Her new book, *Point-No-Point*, will be published this summer by FutureCycle Press.

David Blair is the author of three books of poetry: *Ascension Days* (Del Sol Press, 2007), *Friends with Dogs* (Sheep Meadow Press, 2016), and *Arsonville* (New Issues Poetry & Prose, 2016). He lives in Somerville. Visit his website at http://www.davidblairpoetry.com.

Michael Brosnan, fresh from the Colrain Poetry Conference, is at work putting together his first collection of poetry. His poems have appeared in *Confrontation, Borderlands, Prairie Schooner, Barrow Street, Rattle*, and other journals. By day, he edits *Independent School*, an award-winning magazine on precollegiate education. His book, *Against the Current* (Heinemann) was the basis for the 2009 documentary *Accelerating America*. He lives with his family in Exeter, New Hampshire.

Mary Buchinger is the author of *Aerialist* (Gold Wake) and *Roomful of Sparrows* (Finishing Line). Her poems have appeared in *AGNI, Cortland Review, DIAGRAM, Fifth Wednesday, Nimrod International Journal of Prose and Poetry, The Massachusetts Review*, and elsewhere. She is co-President of the New England Poetry Club, Cambridge Poetry Ambassador, and teaches writing and communication studies at MCPHS University in Boston, Mass.

Philip E. Burnham, Jr. is the author of five books of poetry. He has twice received the Gretchen Warren Award from the New England Poetry Club and was the winner of the Loft Poetry Prize, and the New England Prize from *The Lyric*. His sixth book, *Winter Dreams*, was published by Ibbetson Street Press in December 2015. His website is pebjr.com.

Ruth Chad is a psychologist who lives and works in the Boston area. Her poems have appeared in the *Aurorean, Bagels with the Bards, Ibbetson Street, The Psychoanalytic Couple and Family Institute of New England, Connection, Constellations* and several others. Her chapbook, *The Sound of Angels* is pending publication by Cervena Barva Press in 2016.

Llyn Clague is a poet based in Hastings-on-Hudson, New York. His poems have been published widely, including in *Ibbetson Street, Atlanta Review, Wisconsin Review, California Quarterly, Main Street Rag, New York Quarterly,* and other magazines. His seventh book, *Hard-Edged and Childlike*, was published by Main Street Rag in September, 2014. Visit www.llynclague.com.

Beatriz Alba Del Rio is bilingual poet, lawyer, mediator, member of the New England Poetry Club and of the Bagels Bard. Beatriz' has received everal awards: Octavio Paz, Pablo Neruda, Cambridge Poetry Award, New England Poetry Club: Diana Der-Hovanessian Translation Award. Her poetry has appeared in several anthologies and literary magazines. Beatriz' inspiring muses are Chejov, Borges, Paz, Neruda, Gelman, Jorie Graham. Her poetry guru is Ottone Riccio. Her contemporary poets ingnite Beatriz' light and darkness to write. She believes in the oneness of us all.

Kirk Etherton works as a freelance ad writer, and has done award-winning work for a wide variety of clients. He also coordinates, promotes, and hosts all kinds of events—including the Boston National Poetry Month Festival, of which he is a board member. In addition, Kirk writes and performs music, creates and exhibits art, and teaches English as a foreign language. He can be reached at kirketherton@gmail.com.

Richard J. Fein has published eight books of poetry and two books of translations of Yiddish poetry. *Not a Separate Surge,* his new and selected poems, is forthcoming. He has also published a memoir of Yiddish, *The Dance of Leah*; a book of personal essays, *Yiddish Genesis;* and a critical study, *Robert Lowell.* He lives in Cambridge, Massachusetts.

Peter Fulton has written verse dramas—*Death of A Worn Man, waking dolphins, ordination, How to Carve an Angel;* poems—*Boulders in Ice;* poems and photographs w/sculpture by McAlister Coleman—*Figures*; novella w/poems and music—*Silicon in Sand;* and an interactive poetry multimedia ebook—*flying stones.*

Timothy Gager is the author of eleven books of short fiction and poetry. His latest, *The Thursday Appointments of Bill Sloan*, (Big Table Publishing) is his first novel. He has hosted the successful Dire Literary Series in Cambridge, Massachusetts for over thirteen years and is the co-founder of Somerville News Writers Festival. His work appears in over 300 journals, and ten of his pieces have been nominated for the Pushcart Prize. His work has been read on National Public Radio.

Brendan Galvin is the author of seventeen collections of poems. *Habitat: New and Selected Poems 1965-2005* (LSU Press) was a finalist for the National Book Award. His Cape Cod crime novel, *Wash-a-shores*, is available on Amazon Kindle. *The Air's Accomplices*, a collection of new poems, is available from LSU Press. Galvin lives in Truro, Massachusetts.

Harris Gardner has been published in *The Harvard Review, Midstream, Cool Plums, Rosebud, Fulcrum, Chest, The Aurorean, Ibbetson Street, Main Street Rag, Levure Litteraire* (France, U.S., Germany), *Vallum* (Canada), and over 50 other publications. He was the poet-in-residence at Endicott College from 2002-2005; has been the poetry editor of *Ibbetson Street* since 2010; is the co-founder of Tapestry of Voices and the Boston National Poetry Month Festival (both with Lainie Senechal); and he has been a member of three Poet Laureate selection committees, two in Boston and one in Somerville. He also received the Ibbetson Street Lifetime Achievement Award and a Citation from Massachusetts House of Representatives, both in 2015.

Danielle Legros Georges is the current Poet Laureate of the City of Boston and the author of two books of poems, *The Dear Remote Nearness of You* and *Maroon.* She is a professor in the Creative Arts in Learning Division of Lesley University. Her poems have been widely anthologized, and recent essays of hers have appeared in *Others Will Enter the Gates: Immigrant Poets on Poetry, Influences and Writing in America* and *Anywhere But Here: Black Intellectuals in the Atlantic World and Beyond.*

William Harney is a Professor of English at Endicott College. His work has appeared in *Ibbetson Street, Lyrical Somerville* and elsewhere.

Daniel A. Harris has published two books of poems (*Random Unisons,* 2013; *LooseParlance,* 2008), as well as critical studies of Yeats, Hopkins, and Tennyson. Nominated for a Pushcart award, his poems have been nationally published. Daniel is also an active environmentalist currently focusing on regional land-use issues, sustainable urban planning, and plastic bag reduction. Visit his website, where you can see/hear him read his poems: www.danielharrispoet.net.

Richard Hoffman is author of the *Half the House: a Memoir*, and the poetry collections, *Without Paradise, Gold Star Road,* winner of the 2006 Barrow Street Press Poetry Prize and the 2008 Sheila Motton Award from the New England Poetry Club, and *Emblem*. A fiction writer as well, his *Interference & Other Stories* was published in 2009. His most recent work is the memoir, *Love & Fury*. He is Senior Writer in Residence at Emerson College in Boston.

Lucy Holstedt is a professor at Berklee College of Music and founding director of the Women Musicians Network, which presents their 20th concert at the BPC in November 2016. As board member of the Boston National Poetry Month Festival, Lucy designs and manages the Festival website, bostonnationalpoetry.org, and produces an annual concert of poetry with music and dance. Besides writing poetry and lyrics, Lucy composes and performs choral and solo music in jazz, pop, rock, contemporary classical and comedic styles.

Paul Hostovsky's eighth book of poems, *The Bad Guys*, won the FutureCycle Poetry Book Prize for 2015. His poems have also won a Pushcart Prize, two Best of the Net awards, the Muriel Craft Bailey Award from *The Comstock Review*, and have been featured on *Poetry Daily, Verse Daily,* and *The Writer's Almanac.* To read more of his work, visit him at paulhostovsky.com.

Robert K. Johnson, now retired, was a Professor of English at Suffolk University in Boston for many years. For eight years, he was also the Poetry Editor of *Ibbetson Street* magazine. His poems have been published individually in a wide variety of magazines and newspapers here and abroad. The most recent collections of his poetry are *Flowering Weeds* and *Choir Of Day*.

George Kalogeris teaches English Literature and Classics in Translation at Suffolk University in Boston, Massachusetts. He is the author of a book of paired poems in translation, *Dialogos (Antilever, 2012)*, and of a book of poems based on the life and notebooks of Albert Camus, *Camus: Carnets (Pressed Wafer, 2006)*. His poems and translations have been anthologized in *Joining Music with Reason,* (chosen by Christopher Ricks, Waywiser, 2010).

Barbara Claire Kasselmann is a poet/photographer/ journalist whose poetry credits include *Kalliope, The Worcester Review, Sojourner, Slipstream, Pig Iron, Atlanta Review, Paramour, Marblehead,* other journals and audio tapes. She has received awards from New England Poetry Club and *Atlanta Review*, and taught 14 years at Northeastern University. She published regularly in *The Boston Globe* and many newspapers and magazines.

Judy Katz-Levine's books include *When The Arms Of Our Dreams Embrace* (Saru 1991), *Ocarina* (Saru/Tarsier 2006) and *When Performers Swim, The Dice Are Cast* (Ahadada 2009). Chapbooks include *The Umpire, And Other Masks* (5 Trees Press), *Carpenter* (Firefly), and *Speaking With Deaf-Blind Children* (Free Beginning). Her poems have appeared recently in *Ibbetson Street, Salamander, Gravel, Muddy River Poetry Review, Poem Of The Moment, Miriam's Well, Ygdrasil,* and *Blue Unicorn*. She gives readings in the Boston area. Also a jazz flutist, she works to synthesize the lyricism and depth of improvisational music in her poems.

Lisa D. Kaufman is a visual artist, a poet and a yoga teacher. Her poems have been published in several print and online publications, including the *"Lyrical Somerville"* column of *The Somerville News*, Somerville, Massachusetts, *Bagels with the Bards: Anthology Number 4/Number 5/Number 6*, and *Wilderness House Literary Review*.

X. J. Kennedy's most recent books are *In a Prominent Bar in Secaucus: New & Selected Poems* (Johns Hopkins University Press), *Fits of Concision: Collected Poems of Six or Fewer Lines* (Grolier Poetry Press), and a comic novel, *A Hoarse Half-human Cheer* (Curtis Brown Unlimited). He has received the Jackson Poetry Prize from Poets & Writers and the Robert Frost gold medal from the Poetry Society of America.

Tim Kinsella is an American Sign Language interpreter who lives with his family in eastern Massachusetts. This is his first publication.

Lawrence Kessenich won the 2010 Strokestown International Poetry Prize. His poetry has been published in *Sewanee Review, Atlanta Review, Poetry Ireland Review,* and many other magazines. He has published a chapbook, *Strange News*, and two full-length books, *Before Whose Glory* and *Age of Wonders*. His first novel, *Cinnamon Girl*, will be published in September 2016. His books and his blog, "Writing as a Habit of Being," can be found at www.lawrence-writer.com.

Ted Kooser's most recent books are *Splitting an Order,* poems from Copper Canyon Press, *The Wheeling Year*, prose vignettes from University of Nebraska Press and *The Bell in the Bridge*, a children's book from Candlewick Press. He lives in rural Nebraska and teaches writing at The University of Nebraska.

Susan LaFortune is a poet and writer from Haverhill, Massachusetts. Her first chapbook, *Talking in my Sleep* was published by Finishing Line Press in 2013 and nominated for a pushcart prize. Her work has appeared in various publications including *Muddy River Poetry Review*. You can find her reading her work around the Merrimack Valley and North Shore areas. Find out where she will be next on her Facebook page or contact her at Susanwriteseverything@gmail.com.

Tom Laughlin is a professor at Middlesex Community College in Massachusetts where he teaches creative writing, literature, and composition courses. He was a founding editor of *Vortext*, a literary journal of Massasoit Community College, and a staff reader for ten years at *Ploughshares*. His poetry has appeared in *Green Mountains Review*, *North Essex Review*, and other small journals and magazines.

Kathleen Lentz spent six years in graduate school studying Chinese language, poetry and history, and also writing poetry and fiction. Then she changed course and went to medical school, eventually becoming a child psychiatrist. She sees kids and adults in her therapy practice in Concord, Mass. In recent years she's been making more time for writing and has had work published in *Green Hills Literary Lantern* and the *Arlington Advocate*. She lives in Arlington with her husband and two cats.

Lyn Lifshin's new books include *Knife Edge & Absinthe: the Tango poems; For the Roses, poems for Joni Mitchell, All The Poets Who Touched Me; A Girl Goes Into The Woods; Malala, Tangled as the Alphabet: The Istanbul Poems. : Secretariat: The Red Freak, The Miracle; Malala* and *Femina Eterna: Enheduanna, Scheherazade and Nefertiti; Stained Glass, Maple Leaves. web site:www.lynlifshin.com.*

Fred Marchant is the author of five books of poetry, the most recent of which, *Said Not Said*, is forthcoming from Graywolf Press is 2017. He is an Emeritus Professor of English at Suffolk University in Boston, where he founded the Creative Writing Program and the Poetry Center. He continues to teach workshops in many venues, including the Colrain Poetry Manuscript Conference, the Fine Arts Work Center in Provincetown and the Joiner Institute for the Study of War and Social Consequences at UMass Boston.

Triona McMorrow lives in Dunlaoghaire, County Dublin. She was shortlisted for the International Francis Ledwidge Poetry competition in 2009 and 2011. She was shortlisted for The Galway University Hospitals Arts Trust poetry competition in 2013. She has had poems published in *Ibbetson Street* journal in Boston, Massachusetts. In 2014, The Bealtaine group, of which she is a member, published an anthology of poetry titled *Bealtaine*.

Ed Meek's third book of poems, *Spy Pond*, was published in 2015 by Prolific Press. His collection of stories, *Luck*, is coming out in 2017 with Tailwinds Press. Ed has had poetry, fiction and articles in *The Paris Review, The North American Review, The Boston Globe*, etc. Follow him on Twitter @emeek. His website is edmeek.net.

David P. Miller's chapbook, *The Afterimages*, was published in 2014 by Červená Barva Press. His poems have appeared in *Meat for Tea, Painters and Poets, Fox Chase Review, Wilderness House Literary Review, Autumn Sky Poetry Daily, Oddball Magazine, Incessant Pipe*, and *Muddy River Poetry Review*, among others. His poem "Kneeling Woman and Dog" is included in the 2015 edition of *Best Indie Lit New England*. David is a librarian at Curry College in Milton, Massachusetts.

Alfred Nicol's new collection of poetry, *Animal Psalms*, was published by Able Muse Press in March of this year. His previous collection, *Elegy for Everyone*, was chosen for the first Anita Dorn Memorial Prize in 2009. Nicol received the 2004 Richard Wilbur Award for an earlier volume, *Winter Light*. Nicol's poems have appeared in *Poetry, The Hopkins Review, Dark Horse, First Things, The New England Review, Commonweal, The Formalist*, and other literary journals, as well as in *Contemporary Poetry of New England* and other anthologies.

Tomas O'Leary—poet, translator, music-maker, singer, artist and expressive therapist—has a volume of New & Selected Poems from Lynx House Press: *In the Wellspring of the Ear*. His previous books of poetry are *Fool at the Funeral, The Devil Take a Crooked House*, and *A Prayer for Everyone*. A teacher for many years (college, high school, elementary, adult ed), he has worked (played) the past couple decades with folks who have Alzheimer's, eliciting cognitive and emotional responses through songs, stories, poems, and free-wheeling conversation.

Marge Piercy's 19th poetry book *Made in Detroit* was recently bought by Knopf along with the paperback, *The Hunger Moon: New & Selected Poems 1980-2010*. Piercy has published 17 novels , most recently *Sex Wars;* PM Press republished *Dance the Eagle to Sleep, Vida* and *Braided Lives*, with new introductions, and her first short story collection, *The Cost of Lunch, Etc.*, now in paperback. Her memoir is *Sleeping with Cats*, with Harper Perennial. Her newest nonfiction book is *My Life, My Body*.

Denise Provost has published in on-line and print journals, including Bagel Bards anthologies, *Ibbetson Street, Muddy River Poetry Review, qarrtsiluni, Quadrille, Poetry Porch's Sonnet Scroll, Sanctuary*, and *Light Quarterly*. Provost lives in Somerville, Massachusetts, and does a lot of writing on the Red Line of the MBTA.

Gary Rainford is the author of the poetry collection *Salty Liquor*. Gary lives with his wife and daughter year-round on a small island six miles off the north coast of Maine. Former Artist-in-Residence at Acadia National Park, Gary has had his poetry published in a wide range of literary magazines and university journals, including *North Dakota Quarterly, Aurorean, Kindred*, and, most recently, *Take Heart: More Poems From Maine*, an anthology edited by Wesley McNair. (www.garyrainford.com)

Rene Schwiesow is co-host for the popular South Shore Poetry venue The Art of Words. She has been published in various small press publications including *The Waterhouse Review, Muddy River Poetry Review, City Lights*, Bagel Bards Anthologies and Tidepool Poets Anthologies. She is the author of two poetry chapbooks, with a third book coming soon from Cervena Barva Press.

Bridget Seley-Galway, an artist/poet, has exhibited throughout New England, and can also be seen on the Spanish Island Ibiza's web site. Her poetry has been printed in *Provincetown* Magazine 2009-2010,Bagel Bards Anthology 2009-2012, and Popt Art 2011-2012. Her art has been presented in 1985 *Artist* Magazine, 1991 The Review *Cape Cod Arts and Antiques*, 2005 *Cape Arts Review*, and picked for the covers of Bagel Bards Anthology #5, *Ibbetson Street* #26-#30.

Lainie Senechal, poet, painter and environmentalist, has read and featured at many venues throughout New England. Her poetry has appeared in journals and anthologies including *The Aurorean, Ibbetson Street, Spare Change, Wilderness House Literary Review, The Larcom Review,* and four anthologies. She co-authored two volumes of poetry, *Naiad's Lantern* with Donna and Laura Senechal and *Challice of Eros* with Harris Gardner. Her recent chapbook is V*ocabulary of Awakening.* She is the first Poet Laureate of Amesbury, Massachusetts.

Zvi A. Sesling is a prize winning poet. He edits *Muddy River Poetry Review,* publishes *Muddy River Books* and reviews for *Boston Small Press and Poetry Scene.* He is author of *King of the Jungle* (Ibbetson Street Press, 2010), *Across Stones of Bad Dreams* (Cervena Barva Press, 2011) and *Fire Tongue* (Cervena Barva Press, 2016). He lives in Brookline, Massachusetts with his wife Susan Dechter.

Wendell Smith is a physician who lives in Melrose. His poetry has appeared in *Kansas Quarterly, Constellation, View Northwest* and elsewhere. He won the American Academy of Poets and Sidney Cox Prizes at Dartmouth College where he met Ramon Guthrie in the '60's. He thinks Guthrie's *Maximum Security Ward* should be to 20th century poetry what Moby Dick is to 19th century fiction. If he were in the last chapter of *Fahrenheit 451* memorizing literature, he would memorize Guthrie.

Ruth Smullin lives in the Boston area. Her poetry has appeared in *Common Ground Review, Constellations, Crucible* (winner of the Sam Ragan Prize), *Ibbetson Street, Plainsongs, Sow's Ear Poetry Review* and *The Aurorean.*

Kathleen Spivack is the author of ten books of prose and poetry (Doubleday, Graywolf, and others.) Her most recent, *Unspeakable Things,* is a novel published by Alfred A.Knopf in 2016. The memoir, *With Robert Lowell and His Circle: Sylvia Plath, Anne Sexton, Elizabeth Bishop, Stanley Kunitz and Others,* was published by the University Press of New England, 2012. For more information, go to www.kathleenspivack.com

T. Michael Sullivan has directed the annual Writers' Workshop sponsored by the William Joiner Institute for the Study of War and Social Consequences at the University of Massachusetts Boston since its inception in 1987. Prior to that, he was a high school English teacher and a journalist, winning regional and national awards as editor of the *Somerville Journal.* Subsequently, he was a humor columnist, syndicated among community newspapers. In addition to poetry, he writes humorous rap songs.

Simrin Tamhane is an international student from Sikkim in Northeast India and is currently a sophomore at Endicott College. She is majoring in International Studies and is interested in human rights and a lot of her creative writing is based on her interest in this subject. She enjoys old music, tragedies and lemonade in the winter.

Sandra Thaxter did undergraduate studies in French, German and Russian and graduate studies in Comparative Literature at Indiana University and French at Boston University. She has been a software engineer at Lotus, IBM and other companies, and now directs a non-profit that brings learning programs to rural children in Kenya. She studied poetry at the Blue Heron program in Antigonish, Nova Scotia and in New York City at the 92nd Street Y and the Poetry Project at St. Mark's Church.

Teisha Dawn Twomey is the poetry editor at *Night Train,* as well as an associate fiction editor for Wilderness House Literary Press. She received her MFA in Poetry at Lesley University. Her poetry and short stories have appeared in numerous print and online poetry reviews and journals. By day, she is the Resource Specialist at Springfield College's Boston campus and, by night, she is (currently) at work on her first novel.

Joyce Wilson is creator and editor of the Internet magazine *The Poetry Porch* (www.poetryporch.com), which has been online since 1997. Her poems have appeared in many literary journals, among them *Salamander, Alabama Literary Review, The Lyric,* and *Mezzo Cammin.* Her first book, *The Etymology of Spruce,* and a chapbook, *The Springhouse,* appeared in 2010.